I0817147

Thank You FOR BEING A Teacher!

Keepsake Gift Book

A Gift For:

____

From:

____

When I was very young, most of my childhood heroes wore capes, flew through the air, or picked up buildings with one arm . . . But as I grew, my heroes changed, so that now I can honestly say that anyone who does anything to help a child is a hero to me.

—Fred Rogers

It goes like this: teaching is touching life.

—Jaime Escalante, American educator

I always say that the young people are the future of the world, and if we start with them first, if we educate and develop a sense of tolerance among them, our future, the future of this world, will be in good hands for generations to come.

—Erin Gruwell, American educator and co-author of *The Freedom Writers Diary*

Teaching is not just a job.
It is a human service,
and it must be thought
of as a mission.

—Ralph Tyler, American educator and pioneer of educational evaluation

The greatest sign of success for a teacher . . . is to be able to say, "The children are now working as if I did not exist."

—Maria Montessori, Italian physician and educator; founder of the Montessori method of education

Finish each day and be done with it. You have done what you could. Some blunders and absurdities have crept in; forget them as soon as you can. Tomorrow is a new day. You shall begin it serenely and with too high a spirit to be encumbered with your old nonsense.

—Ralph Waldo Emerson

My heart is singing for joy this morning. A miracle has happened! The light of understanding has shone upon my little pupil's mind, and behold, all things are changed.

—Anne Sullivan, American educator and lifelong companion of Helen Keller

. . . People are the most important part of any classroom. If given the choice between a great teacher and the world's most advanced technology, I'd pick the teacher any day for my own children.

—Sal Khan, American educator and founder of Khan Academy

Once you learn to read,
you will be forever free.

—Frederick Douglass

Everyone who remembers his [or her] own education remembers teachers, not methods and techniques. The teacher is the heart of the educational system.

—Sidney Hook

It is the supreme art of the teacher to awaken joy in creative expression and knowledge.

—Albert Einstein, German-born educator and theoretical physicist

A teacher affects eternity;
[they] can never tell where
[their] influence stops.

—Henry Adams, American educator
and author of *The Education
of Henry Adams*

. . . If I can inspire one of these youngsters to develop the talent I know they possess, then my monument will be in their work.

—Augusta Savage, American sculptor and arts educator of the Harlem Renaissance

Intelligence plus character—that
is the goal of true education.

—Dr. Martin Luther King, Jr.

I'm a teacher. A teacher is someone who leads. There is no magic here. I do not walk on water. I do not part the sea. I just love children.

—Marva Collins, American educator and founder of Westside Preparatory School

An education is not so much about making a living as making a person.

—Tara Westover

Teachers can change lives with just the right mix of chalk and challenges.

—Joyce Meyer

ABC

Education is not the filling of a pail, but the lighting of a fire.

—Plutarch

You will teach them to fly, but they will not fly your flight. You will teach them to dream, but they will not dream your dream. You will teach them to live, but they will not live your life. Nevertheless, in every flight, in every life, in every dream, the print of the way you taught them will remain.

—Mother Teresa

What a teacher is, is more important than what he [or she] teaches.

—Karl Menninger

I touch the future. I teach.
—Christa McAuliffe, American educator and astronaut; first civilian selected for spaceflight

I have come to believe that a great teacher is a great artist, and that there are as few as there are any other great artists. Teaching might even be the greatest of the arts since the medium is the human mind and spirit.

—John Steinbeck

Education is the most powerful weapon which you can use to change the world.

—Nelson Mandela

So much of teaching is sharing. Learning results in sharing, sharing results in change, change is learning.

—Esmé Raji Codell, American educator and author of *Educating Esmé*

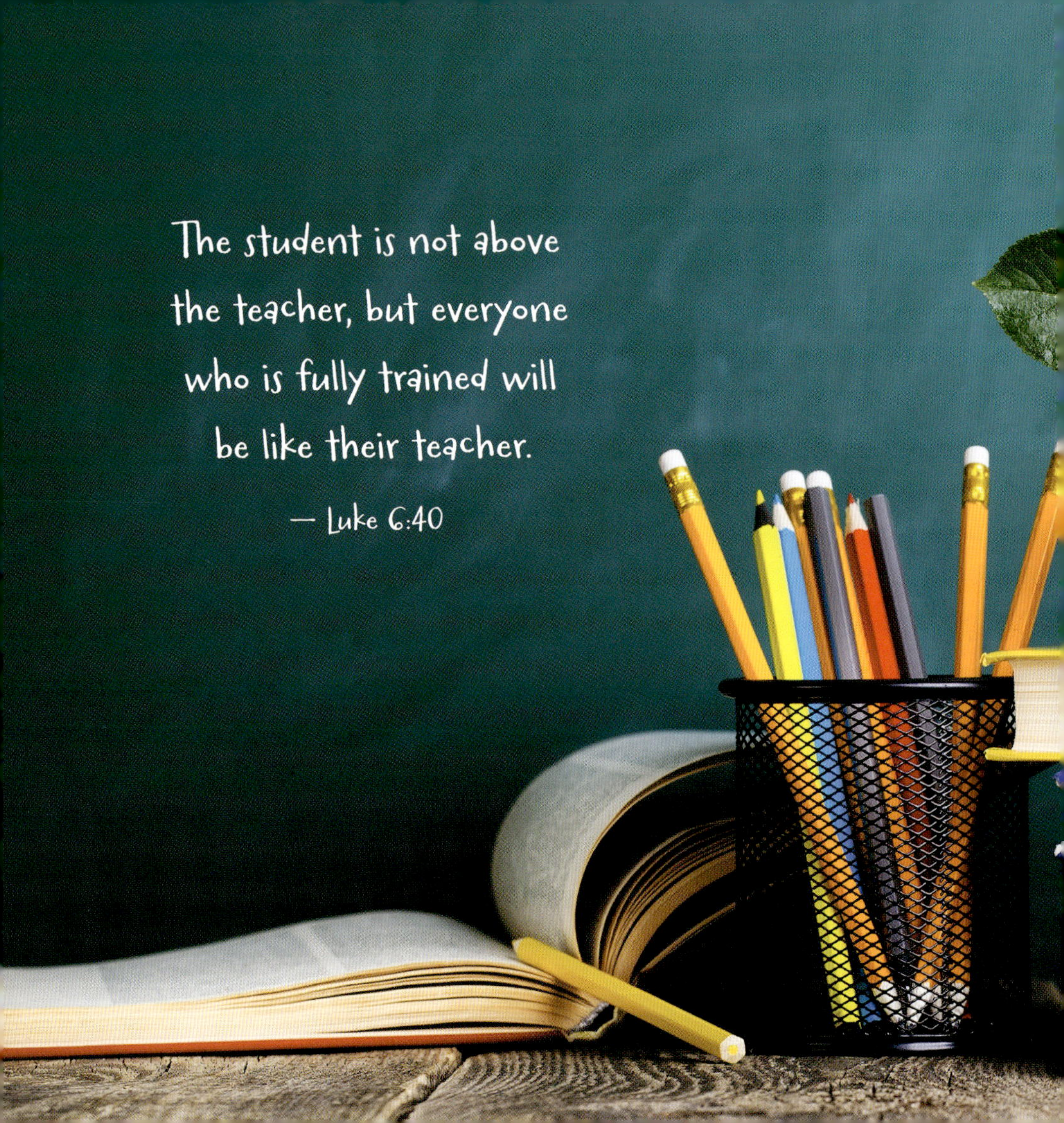
The student is not above
the teacher, but everyone
who is fully trained will
be like their teacher.
— Luke 6:40

Wherever you find something extraordinary,
you'll find the fingerprints of a great teacher.
—Arne Duncan, American educator and
former U.S. Secretary of Education

D
o
n
m
l
o
n

[Teaching is] not supposed to be easy—it's supposed to be worth it.

—Dave Burgess, American educator and author of *Teach like a PIRATE*

When we see the face of a child, we think of the future. We think of their dreams about what they might become, and what they might accomplish.

—Desmond Tutu

The classroom time between teachers and students is magical, and the children deserve to feel that, in that moment, there is nothing more important in the world than their quest for knowledge.

—Ron Clark, American educator and founder of the Ron Clark Academy

I am not a teacher,
but an awakener.

—Robert Frost

Ideal teachers are those who use themselves as bridges over which they invite their students to cross; then, having facilitated their crossing, joyfully collapse, encouraging them to create bridges of their own.

—Nikos Kazantzakis

Images from Shutterstock.com: Africa Studio (cover); aslysun (3); HTWE (5); ForceAlex (7); Julia Shutikova (8–9); locrifa (11); Kittyfly (12–13); Simon Bratt (14–15); hxdbzxy (17); Yuganov Konstantin (18–19, 58–59); Larisa Rudenko (20–21); Oleg Mikhaylov (23); Di Studio (24–25); SUKJAI PHOTO (27); Billion Photos (29); Monkey Business Images (31); Viktor Gladkov (33); pimpampix (35); Vibe Images (36–37); Girkin Photography (39); Mimma Key (40–41); maglara (42–43); Zadorozhnyi Viktor (44–45); Rido (47); Sharomka (49); kozirsky (50–51); Sean Fleming (52–53); Christie Hol (55); Zoteva (56–57); dugdax (60–61); CoCoCholula (62–63).

ISBN 978-1-4971-0602-4

Library of Congress Control Number: 2025917314

Or write to:
Fox Chapel Publishing
903 Square Street
Mount Joy, PA 17552

Printed in China
First printing